SITKA

A Home in the Wild

Photography by Dan Evans ❧ Prose by Carolyn Servid

ISBN: 978-0-578-03179-8

**Books, posters, prints and more
are available at
www.alaskadanevans.com**

All images in this book are available as fine art prints.

Sitka: A Home in the Wild

OLD CAPITAL PRESS

102 Thomas Young Circle, Sitka, Alaska 99835 U.S.A.
Sitkadan@mac.com

Dan Evans: publisher, photographer and editor
Carolyn Servid: writer and editor • Alison Caputo: designer

Library of Congress Control Number: 2009907963

Alaska-wide wholesale distribution by:
Todd Communications
611 E. 12th Ave.
Anchorage, Alaska 99501 U.S.A.
(907) 274-TODD (8633) • sales@toddcom.com
Printed by Everbest Printing Co., Ltd., Nansha, China
through Alaska Print Brokers, Anchorage, Alaska.

I dedicate this book to my son Logan,

who has followed me up mountains

and rivers through muskeg and forest.

Now I am proud to be following you.

A humpback whale breaches in Sitka Sound.

PHOTOGRAPHER'S PREFACE

When I stepped off the jet in Sitka thirty years ago, I had no clue what a grip Baranof Island would have on me. The wilderness was like a magnet pulling me closer and closer, deeper and deeper. This was the place I was looking for. This place was wild. Snow covered peaks, dark forests with giant trees, a volcano that rose above a seemingly endless ocean that stretched all the way to Japan. This was a place I could explore. This was the place I would call home.

How do I explain how I feel about Sitka and its wilderness? This place where my wife and I built our house, raised our son. A place where I have made a living working on airplanes; thinning clear-cuts; loading baggage on jets; commercial fishing for halibut; commercial diving for abalone and sea cucumbers; working as a bicycle mechanic, a carpenter, a home inspector, a store owner, a photographer. This is the place where I have walked through ancient forests, climbed unnamed peaks, swam with sea lions, and soared with the eagles. And there is so much more.

I offer my explanation in the pages of this book—*Sitka: A Home in the Wild*. May the combination of my pictures and Carolyn Servid's prose touch a place in your heart and reflect some of your own feelings about life on this island that holds its secrets deep within.

Kraak! Kraak!
Raven interrupts your sleep.
Summer morning. 5:40. Full daylight floods the sky.
Kraak! The world is awake, alive! Kraak! Kraak!

Eyes closed you listen and imagine raven overseeing his world—the dark spruce and hemlock forests, the ragged stone edges of this island buffeted by the cold waters of the North Pacific, the steep rise of land jutting skyward, moving up past trees to alpine meadows, snowfields, glaciers, topping out in bare rock a mile high above the sea. The Tlingit *Sheet'ka Kwáan* have made this place their home for thousands of years, living on the open sea side of the island renamed much later by Russian colonists after their leader Baranof. *Sitka* the newcomers called the town and call it still.

And raven calls, again, lifts off from his perch, flies out over the town settled on a shelf of land where the *Kaasda Héen* / Indian River valley flattens out the island's edge. On that edge, up against the mountains, Sitka faces the sea and scores of islands that frame Sitka Sound, a pocket of the larger ocean beyond. Raven flies out, takes in the wide view, circles back over the clustered homes and businesses downtown, boats tied safely in harbor, the golden crosses atop the onion dome of St. Michael's Russian Orthodox Cathedral. Here is a place full of people whose hearts are captive to its wild beauty. Raven settles in the cottonwood tree on a knoll above town, calls again commandingly, his voice rebounding as though he were the owner of this grand estate. How lucky we are to share it with him.

The ever-watchful raven takes flight from atop a gnarled hemlock.

People

This is the place we call home.

We fishermen in bibbed rain gear and rubber boots, toughened bodies trained by rolling seas, rituals defined by bait and hook and line, boats seaworthy with care, clothes breathing diesel-fish air, salt air, flashing fish over the gunwale, filling the cooler, filling the hold.

We berrypickers reaching into cool leaves of salmonberry, gently plucking the scarlet-orange-yellow seeded clusters. Hovering at huckleberry, blueberry, filling buckets with crimson and dusky-blue jewels. Keeping the secret patch of nagoons to ourselves. Tables of pies and cobblers, pantries of syrup and jam.

We hunters who follow deer through woods and high mead-

ows, quiet, watchful, waiting for the gift to present itself, taking a life to nurture a life, bone and muscle and blood. We gardeners who nurture soil and seed into potatoes and carrots, lettuce and cabbage, broccoli and beets.

We brightly clad hikers, taking to the woods, loners and friends, parents and children, dogs and dogs. We winterlovers, climbing to alpine slopes, our ski tracks snaking down clean white snow. We who take to the water in skiff and kayak, ever watchful of skies and winds and seas, salt spray in our faces, wave-riding movement in our bones. *Gunalcheesh!*

Gunalcheesh for all that this place provides. *Gunalcheesh!*

Gunalcheesh!

1

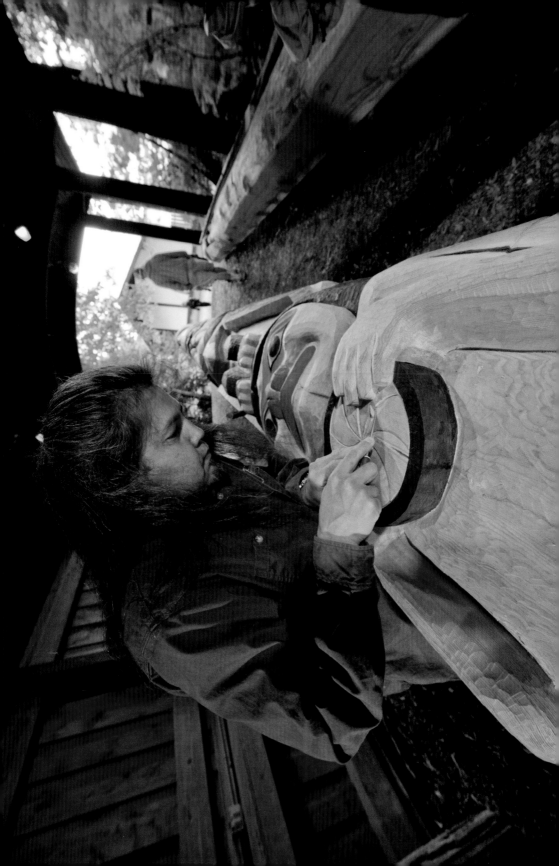

Left: Master Carver Tommy Joseph puts finishing touches on the Michio Hoshino totem pole.

Above: Sitkans join together to raise the Hoshino pole at Halibut Point Recreation Area.

Previous page: The seven-mile hike to the top of Mt. Edgecumbe provides spectacular views of Sitka Sound.

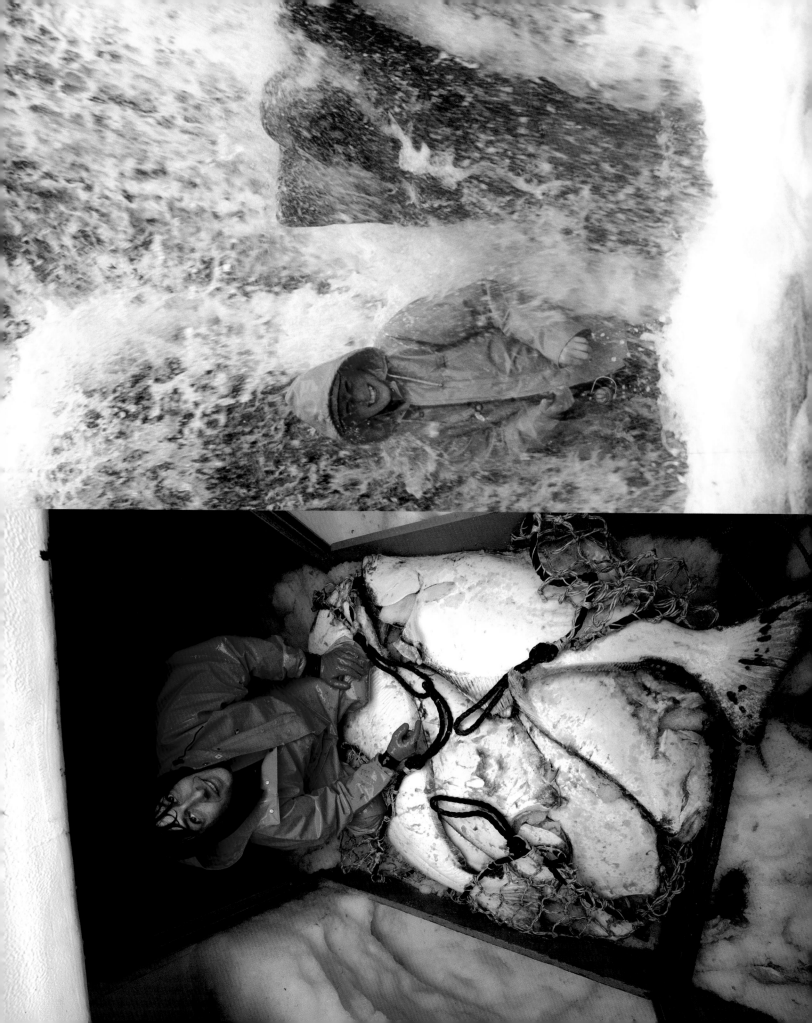

A skier crosses Swan Lake on a cold winter morning.
Left: Jeff Farvour unloading halibut from the fishing vessel Christi Rob.
Brandon Forst and Logan Evans test raingear at Plotnikof Lake.

Feather & Song

Early in March when days are being stretched by returning light,

listen for two clear assurances of spring—winter wren's long chattery song and the single-note whistle of varied thrush. Their voices imbue the still-cool atmosphere with possibility, their solos the opening of a chorus of seasonal birdsong. The air soon fills with junco's trill and song sparrow's morning sparkle, with the excited triplets of ruby crowned kinglet, the squeaky pulley of Townsend's warbler, robin's cheerful chirrup, the chittering of whizzing rufous hummingbirds.

April and early May, go to the shoreline and catch sight of visiting travelers—sandpiper and turnstone, godwit and curlew, dowitcher, yellowlegs, plover, whimbrel. Listen to their chatter, their haunting watery cries. Watch flocks turn

and rise, turn and settle to ground, waves of wings moving as one. Perhaps an unusual Caspian tern stops by, perhaps the rare red knot.

Out on the water migrating scaup and widgeon, northern shoveler and green winged teal swim among more local mergansers and laughing mallards, goldeneyes and buffleheads, the colorful harlequins. Rafts of dark scoters move through. Let your imagination follow them to the far horizon.

As spring moves toward summer, linger with the gentle lyric of hermit thrush. Hold in that clarity. And at solstice, revel in the joyous spiraling song of Swainson's thrush. No human composer could have done better.

Logan Evans with his new found friends, Canadian goslings.
Right: White fronted geese take flight during spring migration north.

Water

Here at the eastern edge of the North Pacific, banks of saturated clouds move onshore,

sweep up Baranof Island's mountain slopes, drop water as drenching rain, as drizzle, as faint mist, as wind blown specks, as easy showers, as the ragged sheets of a storm. It falls and falls, sustaining the magnificent rainforest that drapes itself over the rising land. It confounds human inhabitants who wait weeks for rain to desist, and worry after too many unnaturally dry days.

All that water drips from alder and cedar, spruce needles and hemlock boughs. It saturates soils and muskegs. It collects in droplets on leaf and stem, perfect beads of clarity magnifying blades of grass, veins of dogwood, magenta hue of a rose. It pools up between stones, rambles in small streams, collects

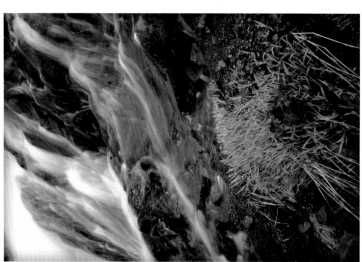

Common red paintbrush near a mountain stream.
Right: Dewdrops on the leaves of Nootka lupine.

in mountain lakes, tumbles off cliffs, hurtles airborne down hundreds of feet, roars at the rocks that break its fall, rushes on over logs and boulders, circles itself in eddies, eases into the river body that flows and flows and flows to meet the salt sea.

We humans walk in the rain, work in the rain, bike in the rain, barbecue in the rain. We tuck ourselves into dry homes and listen to it pound on the roof. We drink up the clouds that fall to earth, nurture ourselves with this clean gift.

The turquoise water of Medvejie Lake.
Right: Indian River Falls.

A large Western hemlock grows at the edge of Sitka Sound.

Right: Car lights streak across the 1,255-foot John O'Connell Bridge in early morning light. Mount Edgecumbe, a dormant volcano, sleeps in the background.

The icy water of the Baranof River roars by a heated pool at Baranof Warm Springs on the east side of the island.

Left: A brown bear fishing for salmon blends into its surroundings.

Forest

Find your way to the old-growth forest and stand with the trees—

the solid dark spruce, the sturdy hemlock. Feel your own height and girth in comparison to theirs. Try to absorb a sense of their years. Imagine them as saplings one, two, five centuries ago. Think about their rooted-ness, their steadfast hold on one particular place. Imagine what they've weathered—storm winds and rains, easy breezes, quiet air, cycles of light, every shade of darkness. Imagine their highest tips reaching skyward far above the branches and filigree of needles. Watch their boughs flutter gently in a breeze. Or stand with them in a gale and listen while their whole bodies sway and thrash, crack, tangle with each other as they move but hold. Try to comprehend their strength. Breathe in their sweet scent.

Standing amongst old-growth Sitka spruce.

Right: A river meanders through dense old-growth forest.

16

Take in the light that filters down between them to the layered understory, green upon green upon green upon green. Devil's club platter-like leaves spread out above blueberry, huckleberry, menzesia, dogwood, bramble, foamflower, carpet of deer heart, carpet of mosses, carpet of fern.

Go to the forest and stand still in honor of the trees. Respect is not too much to offer these ancient living beings. Lean your back against an eight-foot diameter spruce. Run your hand over its rough scaly bark. Be grateful for the vital breath it gives back to the earth.

Karl Wolfe skiing the trees on Mount Verstovia.

Left: Totem poles blend into the forest at Sitka National Historical Park.

Estuary & Muskeg

Estuary. At water's edge, where stream meets inlet,

the summer green of Lyngby's sedge creates an essential feeding zone of this coastal rainforest. Watch here for moving forms, the humped back of a brown bear. Look again: not one but four, a sow and yearling cubs, grazing on this protein-rich beach plant. The sow raises her head, sees you now at safe boat-distance, watches you, her eyes keen in her large round face. Assured, she goes back to eating, young ones ambling,

munching beside her. Summer light glistens, turns her brown fur golden. Imagine her strength as she moves, muscles rippling down her broad back, her massive legs. Try to absorb the beauty of her power.

Down the beach a safe several hundred yards, sharpen your focus on a smaller more delicate form, the fine lines of a Sitka black-tail deer, head raised, chewing a mouth full of

A young brown bear fords the river at Port Banks.

Muskeg. At the forest's edge, this welcome opening, this space defined by an uninterrupted stretch of sky above and spongy wet bog underfoot. Sphagnum moss blanketing a deep layer of peat that has accumulated here for thousands of years. The wide reach is dotted with stunted and gnarled gray-barked shore pines and dark muddy ponds of standing brown water.

Set foot on this ancient history and your boot squishily sinks into soft water-logged

Lyngby's sedge. The doe watches you too, dark eyes and black nose framing the triangle of her face, ears cocked toward you, listening. Wary, she holds her gaze, her body still, gauging her own safety each moment until your proximity signals danger. She steps tentatively first, then prances lightly out of the sedge toward the forest up the beach. Watch her delicate legs carry her away, catch the flick of her tail as she disappears into the trees.

A bouquet of flowers on the forest floor: Canadian dwarf dogwood, Western bog-laurel, mountain buttercup.

Left: Dwarf dogwood blooms in a Harbor Mountain muskeg.

tussocks. Step carefully and walk out into the openness. Take time to crouch down and look at the marvels at your feet, dense congregations of plants specially adapted to the muskeg's nutrient-poor waters and soils. Intricately branching reindeer lichen, waxy-leaved crowberry, pink bog laurel, sticky false asphodel. The happy-looking sundew haloed with fine red hairs oozing sticky fluid to trap insects. Or the purple-flowered butterwort whose slimy leaves do the same. The crowd of color—yellows and browns and reds in the green moss, here the pink-tinged blueberry flower, here the white clustered blossom of Labrador tea. Straighten your back and knees, stand still, look around. You'll find yourself surrounded by a comforting quiet, embellished perhaps by thrush song—the varied's trilled whistle, the hermit's flute in the distance—deepening the calm that settles here.

When low tides uncover the islands' beaches and rocky shores, let yourself meander amidst the marvel and color of the under-water world.

Beach & Rocky Shores

Beachcombers at Shelikof Bay.

Left: A common murre flies to its rookery nest on Saint Lazaria Island.

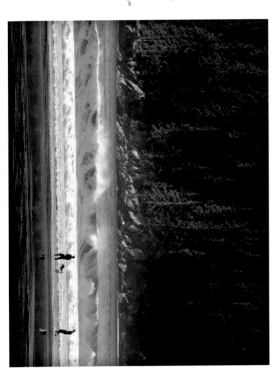

Blooming yarrow above the glacier-fed water of Takatz Bay.

Left: Fireweed blooms along a beach near Sitka.

Next pages:

Left: First light catches a bald eagle on a rocky shore near Sitka.

Right: A campfire glows under a spectacular night sky.

Find a rocky outcrop and linger over a tide pool coated with pink algae. Dip your hand in and gently move aside hairy seaweed and blades of kelp, then allow your eyes to focus: green sea anemone, spiny urchins, hermit crabs, darting sculpin, periwinkles, tube worms with red feather-duster tentacles asway, limpets and chitons stuck fast to stone. On broken barnacle-encrusted rock, purple and orange starfish, squished in crevices, draped over edges, arms spread or tangled or curled. Miniature red sponge volcanoes creating their own landscape.

Imagine the wash of waves here, the weight of the water pushing, pulling, the rush of noise. Imagine the scene at high tide, sunlight filtering down through watery green, through wavering blades of kelp and algae, all this exquisite life out of our sight, at home in the depths.

Here, a bed of emerald eel grass, shining wet blades all laid down in one direction. Atop the green, the purple burst of a grand sunflower star, fiery red moving down its umpteen legs. Or here a sandy stretch covered with yellower-green sea lettuce, dotted with clam holes, squirting shots of water arcing into the air. Listen to the chorus of wet noise—burbling, sucking, slurping, popping, bubbling, crunching, squealing.

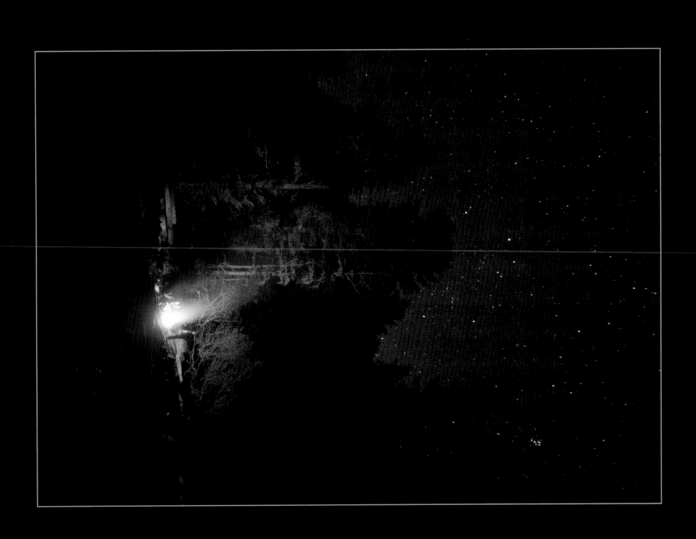

As long as people have been living on this island, salmon have been returning to its rivers and streams.

As long as people have known this land, salmon have inhabited their stories. As long as people have subsisted here, salmon have been essential food. This place and its cultures are infused with salmon, whole watersheds and their inhabitant species—spruce, hemlock, bear, otter, eagle, raven, and others—are nourished by salmon. Households live year-round on salmon. Baked, poached, sautéed, in chowders and soups, dips and omelettes, it is both staple and delicacy.

salmon

Cal Hayashi holds up a winter king salmon caught near Sitka.

Right: A salmon troller rounds the corner of the volcanic island of Saint Lazaria.

Fisherman's best friend.
Left: Fishermen pull in a seine net loaded with salmon.

Seagulls crowd the beaches and air during the spring herring spawn. Fishermen net the herring for bait fish.

Right: Boats rest quietly moored in Eliason Harbor as a full moon glows above Mount Edgecumbe.

Next pages:

Left: Herring spawn by the millions in Sitka Sound during the spring.

Right: Ian Kott flies high above Sitka Sound in his paraglider. Spawning herring have turned the water below a tropical turquoise.

Late spring, when word spreads about kings off Biorka, off the Cape, off Vitskari. anglers rig up their boats and head out. The season's first fresh salmon is the sweetest, shared in gratitude with family, friends, perfectly-grilled chinook. You savor its tender flesh, lick delectable oil off your fingers. Soon trollers are baiting hooks, seiners readying their nets. Harbors empty out and holds begin to fill with flashing silver, these beautiful creatures that nurture our well-being. Subsistence gatherers share the stream's bounty with bears, dipnetting their catch. All over town, people are putting up fish, filling boxes, freezers, smokers, and jars. Each fall, when rivers are filled with salmon coming home to stay, give thanks to these life-givers—king and coho, sockeye, pink and chum—ocean adventurers, bright swimmers of the sea.

Alpine

Up where edges sharpen against thin air,

where blue summer lupine spreads across slanting meadows, where winter smoothes angled mountainsides to snow fields iced in by cornice and ridge; up where the land falls steeply down slope, off precipice; up where your silhouette becomes part of the line that cuts into the sky, where the horizon stretches so far away that you can begin to see the curvature of the earth, you can begin to sense yourself on its surface, small in the immense openness, keenly alive on this high rim of the world.

Shooting stars bloom against a lichen-covered rock.

Right: A skier and snow-boarder hike above tree line on Mount Verstovia to enjoy a day of fun in the powder.

Perhaps in summer you lie down amidst the wild flowers, perhaps you find a stone seat that affords you views of the crowded spruce and hemlock below, the order created by Sitka's streets and houses and harbors, and beyond, the dark islands breaking up the glinting water of Sitka Sound. Perhaps you look down on an eagle soaring on rising air. Perhaps, after a winter climb up, you strap skis or snowboard to your feet and launch yourself down, snow flying around you, behind you, energy and speed awakening every part of your being.

High on the mountain there is a sense of freedom not available down below, as though all that falls away beneath your gaze leaves you unburdened, lightened, being that much closer to the sky.

On a hike across Baranof Island, hikers and their dogs check out the blue pool at the edge of a three-mile long glacier.
Right: A hiker above an unnamed lake on Baranof Island.
Previous page: Lupines bloom in the alpine above Lake Diana.
Next page: A waxing moon and summer sunset over Sitka Sound.

Whale

When the steamy spout of whale-hot breath bursts skyward, your eye goes to it

and stays in the space of anticipation left behind. Perhaps that misty spout drifted toward you and you took it into your own lungs, sharing essential breath with this leviathan whose back now rises, gleaming wet, black, arcing as it moves forward, then sinks under water. You wait now, eyes on the surface, ears keen. But what comes next is no spout of hot air but the whole whale—snout, head, body surging skyward, flippers spread like wings

A kayaker in Eastern Channel paddles over the smooth "footprint" left by a diving humpback whale. In the distance, two other humpbacks raise their flukes to dive deep for their fill of herring.

Right: A large orca whale plows through the water in search of food.

48

Four adult orcas and a young one swim through Chatham Strait in search of salmon.

Left: Humpback whales work in concert bubble-net feeding for small fish. Diving below their prey, they blow a giant ring of encircling bubbles, then swim straight to the surface in the center of the net, mouths wide open to take in the feast.

that would let it fly, a full breach, over as quickly as it began, forty massive tons hitting water that explodes with impact. Your startled heart thunders, your breath halts in amazement, your skin prickles with goose bumps. You reluctantly let your exhilaration settle as the water quiets to easy waves. The breeze whistles in your ears, gulls cry. And then the whale rises again, lazily, its

steamy exhalation lingering over the water, its back rising, rising in the high arc that raises its wide flukes, its signature, specific in shape and markings. You want to memorize every detail as the enormous tail slides into the water, find yourself staring into the smoothed-surface footprint left behind, your mind following the whale down, down, down in its deep dive.

Aurora Borealis & the Night Sky